MINIATURE RAILWAYS

David Henshaw

SHIRE PUBLICATIONS

Bloomsbury Publishing Plc

Kemp House, Chawley Park, Cumnor Hill, Oxford OX2 9PH, UK

29 Earlsfort Terrace, Dublin 2, Ireland

1385 Broadway, 5th Floor, New York, NY 10018, USA

E-mail: shire@bloomsbury.com

www.shirebooks.co.uk

SHIRE is a trademark of Osprey Publishing Ltd

First published in Great Britain in 2021

A catalogue record for this book is available from the British Library.

ISBN: PB 978 1 78442 440 4

eBook 978 1 78442 441 1

ePDF 978 1 78442 438 1

XML 978 1 78442 439 8

21 22 23 24 25   10 9 8 7 6 5 4 3 2 1

Typeset by PDQ Digital Media Solutions, Bungay, UK

Printed and bound in India by Replika Press Private Ltd.

COVER IMAGE
Locomotive 7 *Typhoon* of the Romney, Hythe & Dymchurch Railway approaching Hythe station (Alamy). Back cover detail: close-up of Eastleigh Lakeside Miniature Railway locomotive *Channel Packet* (kitmasterbloke/CC BY 2.0).

TITLE PAGE IMAGE
The Exbury Steam Railway (see page 45) must count among the smartest and best-maintained miniature railways in the country, if not the world. The 12¼-inch gauge gives plenty of seating capacity, with relatively modest construction and running costs.

CONTENTS PAGE IMAGE
The final section of the Romney, Hythe & Dymchurch Railway to Dungeness (see page 54) opened in August 1928, and ran through wilder, less populous country, often on the beach itself. In late 2016, *Winston Churchill* crosses the shingle near Romney Sands with an afternoon train.

ACKNOWLEDGEMENTS

Images are acknowledged as follows:

© Andy Norsworthy, pages 47, 48, 49 (top); © Barton House Railway, page 18; © Bob Bullock, pages 10, 11; © Chris Kennedy, page 55; © David Enefer, page 59; © Eastleigh Lakeside Steam Railway, page 37; © Hastings Miniature Railway Archive, pages 39, 40; © Jonathan James, page 33; © Keith Herbert, page 45; © Ken Jones, pages 6, 17; © Marc Humphreys, page 22; © Mike Underwood, page 24; © Nick Warren, page 4; © Peter Wilson, page 13; © Photo by Craig Tiley, PECO, Beer Devon, page 30; © Ravenglass Railway Museum Collection, page 50; © Simon Merrit, page 32; © Steve Andrews/Classic Traction, page 14.

All other images are from the author's own collection.

CONTENTS

INTRODUCTION

THE RAILWAY LITERATURE usually suggests that miniature railways became established in the late Victorian era, but recent research suggests their origins go back a great deal further – indeed, almost as far back as railways themselves. There are few surviving records of early miniature railways and locomotives, but tantalising paragraphs pop up in newspaper reports from the 1840s and 1950s, some fragments of written history have survived, and there are a handful of locomotives.

The thinking behind the very first miniature locomotives is not really known. At the time of writing, the earliest locomotive is thought to have been built by one Charles Albert Leatham around 1840, although why it was made is unclear. Albert was a young man hoping to establish his credentials as a railway engineer, so perhaps we should think of it as a demonstration piece, at a time when recognised engineering qualifications were in their infancy.

This may also apply to the machine built by Robert Pearson Brereton at about the same time. Brereton joined I.K. Brunel's staff in 1836 at the age of 18. As the model is of a well-established locomotive, it's not inconceivable he measured one up and built a model to demonstrate his capabilities, but for various reasons, it's more likely to have been made later. Building it certainly did Brereton no harm, because by the age of 29 he had become Brunel's chief assistant and is credited with supervising the construction of the Royal Albert Bridge at Saltash, completed in 1859.

OPPOSITE
The 1970s heralded the era of a new breed of 7¼-inch railways that were cheap to build and run, carrying more passengers behind very powerful locomotives. The first – and arguably the best – was the Forest Railroad at Dobwalls in Cornwall. This is 4-8-4 *Queen of Wyoming*.

A report in the *Hampshire Chronicle* of 27 March 1843 relates to a miniature railway constructed for Captain Robert Rodney at Alresford in Hampshire. Judging by the purely decorative tunnel, this 400-yard circuit seems to have been built solely for the entertainment of the Captain, his family and guests. Not unusual today, but this was just three years after the completion of the formative London & Southampton Railway, which passed some 8 miles away, and 22 years before the 'grown up' railway reached Alresford! The line seems to have survived for several decades and ended up dual-gauge, with two locomotives and ten items of rolling stock. The Alresford line and other early miniature railways and locomotives were around 12-inch gauge – a bit big by modern standards, but presumably chosen with a shrug as a suitable round figure.

Albert Leatham's model of the Stephenson patent locomotive may have been a demonstrator for prospective employers. It probably dates from the early 1840s.

Such historical fragments tell us very little, and there may have been dozens of others, but we need to skip almost a generation to find more detail. Much better documented are the 15-inch gauge estate railways promoted by Sir Arthur Heywood from the 1870s as the 'minimum gauge' railway, which of course it wasn't then or now, but Sir Arthur was thinking in terms of working estate railways. He could never have guessed that his minimum gauge would become the recognised standard for the largest miniature pleasure lines, of which two appear in this book.

Evolution of narrower gauges, suited to large gardens rather than country estates, seems to have been a bit hit and miss. Pleasure lines were certainly constructed on the Ardkinglas Estate on Loch Fyne, at Far Sawley in Cumbria, and at Chippenham in Wiltshire.

Most of these railways seem to have been quite substantial affairs, except for the Chippenham line, which appears to have been 15-inch gauge.

The first reliably recorded railway of 10¼-inch gauge was built by Sir John C. Holder in the grounds of Pitmaston, his mansion in Moor Green, Birmingham in the late 1890s. Some earlier model locomotives had been built at 9½-inch gauge, because this equated more or less to a scale of 2 inches to the foot, or 1:6, but Sir John's line had that extra ¾ inches and was all the better for it.

There is some debate about how and why this unique 10¼-inch line came about. The strongest theory is that it was constructed around a broad gauge locomotive acquired by the Holders, and (probably) built to the scale of 1½ inches to the foot, or 1:8. Another theory suggests that the builder of this loco had made a common mistake, and set the wheel 'back to back' to 9½ inches, giving a gauge of 10¼ inches, and the Holders scaled everything up to suit. If that really was the case, it wasn't the last time such a mistake would be made,

Sir John Holder's line at Pitmaston, Birmingham was probably the first 10¼-inch railway, the gauge being chosen to suit this 4-2-2 locomotive.

and it certainly wasn't the last time a whole railway (and later derivatives) would be based around a unique locomotive. This seems unlikely though, especially as the handsome 4-2-2 was always known as the 'broad gauge model'. In any event, the Pitmaston Moor Green Railway is regarded as the father of garden lines, and it established scales and practices that have endured into the twenty-first century.

The 10¼-inch might have faded away if Sir John's engineer, John William Grimshaw, hadn't later built his own 10¼-inch line and locomotives at Broome near Stourbridge, adding the stock from Pitmaston when that line closed. In 1903, Henry Greenly – the engineer who would go on to design some of the finest miniature locomotives – settled on 10¼-inch gauge, and that was that. The 10¼-inch miniature railway had arrived as public entertainment.

Origins of the 7¼-inch gauge are more tangled. It has become the predominant gauge for new miniature lines today, so it's generally considered a 1970s innovation, but its origins go back much further. As with 9½-inch, it was very nearly an exact scale of the 4-foot 8½-inch standard gauge, but not quite, because a true match for a scale of 1½ inches to the foot (1:8 scale) would be closer to 7-inch gauge. In 1899 the Society of Model Engineers proposed a range of precise scale-model gauges (at that stage no one really expected to haul passenger trains with such tiny locomotives) of 3¼ inches (1:15), 4⅔ inches (1:12) and 7 inches (1:8). A subcommittee was appointed, but anarchy continued to prevail and in the end the model gauges all ended up slightly different. The failure of 7-inch gauge seems to have been partly down to Henry Greenly who was arguing for 7¼-inch gauge. It's not clear why, but knowing Greenly, the reasoning is more likely to have been about stability or squeezing in a generous firebox than some issue of scale or aesthetics.

In 1908, the model firm of Bassett-Lowke built a 7¼-inch gauge locomotive to the order of a Mr Coates of Paisley, and this was designed by Greenly and proudly displayed in the Bassett-Lowke catalogue with a range of other equipment and rolling stock, thus inadvertently promoting the gauge as a standard, which it really wasn't, although it soon would be.

The 7¼-inch was given a significant boost by one Louis Shaw of Ilkeston, Derbyshire, who built a number of locomotives from 1910, and ran them on the first commercial 7¼-inch miniature railway from 1915, at Little Hallam Reservoir, a local beauty spot. Developments seem to have centred around the East Midlands and South Yorkshire, with a possible garden line in the area from 1906, and the well-documented Saltwood Railway, established in Sheffield from around 1910, later moving with its owner to Saltwood in Kent, where for most of the twentieth century it claimed the title of 'oldest existing miniature railway'. Others would follow, but the gauge wasn't widely adopted until the early 1970s, when it became popular as a cheap 'mass-market' garden format, later achieving similar success in the commercial world, thanks to bigger, more powerful locomotives, and lower, more stable rolling stock.

Until the 1930s, and thanks largely to promotion by Henry Greenly and the Bassett-Lowke company, the accent would

Bassett-Lowke's 15-inch gauge 4-4-2 *Little Giant* (shown here during trials at Eaton Hall) brought the power, performance and sheer grandeur of miniature railways to a new level.

be on 15-inch gauge. Bassett-Lowke built a 'prototype' 4-4-2 Atlantic called *Little Giant* in 1905, which caused something of a sensation, hauling up to 12 tons and hitting 26mph when on trial at the Duke of Westminster's Eaton Hall estate railway in Cheshire. The sheer scale and expense were beyond all but the biggest garden and wealthiest client, but 15-inch gauge was ideal for commercial pleasure lines, and this is when some of the most famous miniature lines were built: Blackpool in 1905, Sutton Coldfield in 1908, both Rhyl and Southport in 1911, the Ravenglass & Eskdale in 1915, Fairbourne in 1916, Margate in 1919, and the Romney, Hythe & Dymchurch in 1927. Against all the odds, most of these have survived as vibrant businesses to this day.

The austerity of the 1930s brought this great era of expansion to a close, with a trend towards smaller and cheaper 10¼-inch gauge railways. These were usually modest seaside affairs, with the glorious exception of the Surrey Border & Camberley Railway (SB&CR), which opened in 1938 on the eve of war. It went from nowhere to nowhere-in-particular,

The Surrey Border & Camberley was a brave experiment to build the biggest 10¼-inch gauge railway, doomed through high operating costs and global conflict to an operating life of just two years.

but it was over 2 miles long and – like the Romney, Hythe & Dymchurch – it was very much a main line in miniature, with long stretches of double track and a fine stable of locomotives. Surrey was wealthy commuter country, but the SB&CR never had a chance to get properly established, and it was doomed to live a short but explosively influential life, dogged by financial losses for two short seasons, then closed with the outbreak of hostilities in September 1939.

Even more so than the First World War, the Second World War decimated all the existing miniature railways. Most seaside resorts were closed and fortified due to invasion fears, and their miniature railways were either mothballed or scrapped, many never to return. A few pleasure lines in industrial areas stayed open with official blessing, presumably as part of the drive to keep war-workers happy. Dudley Zoo (then 10¼-inch gauge, but later 15-inch) was the best known, but survival with a skeleton staff, no coal, little maintenance and curtailed operating hours was probably worse than being mothballed, although they were at least doing their bit.

The SB&CR ran between a grand terminus at Farnborough Green and a more workaday 'country' terminus at Camberley, where the loco sheds were located. Photos from Camberley are rare, and colour is even more special. No.2006 *Edward VIII* prepares to leave Camberley. On the platform, Alexander Kinloch, the owner of the railway, is on the right.

THE GOLDEN ERA

The public were hungry for entertainment after the war, and the new breed of miniature railways usually did a roaring trade, as here at Poole Park in Dorset. The 4-4-2 Atlantic *Vanguard* was built in 1947 to capitalise on the post-war boom.

After more than five years of war, followed by further years of unprecedented austerity, the British public were determined to enjoy themselves, and with plenty of demobbed soldiers looking to earn a few bob, the late 1940s saw a boom in miniature railway construction and reconstruction. Despite shortages of just about everything, locomotives were brought back from the dead, or built from scratch in cold, ill-equipped workshops – often laboriously hand-chiselled from whatever scrap could be begged or borrowed.

Many railways didn't reopen, but pretty well every single item of existing rolling stock was sought out and put to use somewhere. If you could get a serviceable locomotive on the track, the summer seasons of 1947 and beyond were wonderful years. And there were many new railways too, almost all of them

continuing the pre-war 10¼-inch trend: Weymouth in 1947, New Brighton, Cleethorpes, Hastings, Littlehampton, Saltburn and many others in 1948, Poole in 1949, and so on. By the mid-1950s, almost every seaside town or inland tourist honeypot had a railway of some kind, and most were new, or at least recycled, and the majority were 10¼-inch gauge.

A long period of stability followed this rapid expansion. Seaside miniature railways were doing good business, and some were very profitable. There were a few closures, often through muddled thinking and changes of plan by local authorities. But a replacement railway would usually spring up elsewhere in town, and these and other newcomers more than made up for the losses, sad though many of them were. A survey of miniature railways in the mid-1960s would have revealed a healthy mixture of big operations – some now familiar to two or three generations – and many hundreds of smaller 10¼-inch gauge lines, usually in coastal towns. Some of these would already have been well known in the locality, but others were completely new. Altogether, quite a dynamic picture.

But even then, there were worrying signs. Running costs, particularly with coal-fired locomotives, were creeping up, and profitability was (literally) going south, as wealthier, more aspirational holidaymakers began to venture further afield than Bognor or Cleethorpes. It wasn't always obvious on the ground, where visitor numbers often looked buoyant, but the bucket-and-spade holiday was dying, and most miniature railways were tied to the concept.

By 1970, with foreign package holidays getting well into their stride, things were looking bad. Some steam locomotives

Most of the 15-inch gauge railways weathered the 'package holiday' storm, but there were exceptions, such as the Dreamland Miniature Railway, Margate, photographed soon after closure in 1980.

The Forest Railroad's 'Big Boy' *William Jeffers* was one of the biggest and heaviest 7¼-inch locos ever made. It was built by Severn Lamb in 1978 and is pictured here just before closure of the railway in 2006.

were kept running with reduced maintenance, while others were scrapped and replaced by diesels.

Those railways unable to economise simply faded away and died, although this could be a long drawn out and painful affair, and a few ghostly survivors hung on into the 1980s. The biggest and most important lines seemed as busy as ever, but there were closures here too: Rhyl in 1969 (later reopened), and Margate's Dreamland in 1980. Others teetered on the brink. The Ravenglass was very nearly sold for scrap in 1960, but saved by a preservation group, and the Romney, Hythe & Dymchurch survived all manner of vicissitudes, from fatal crashes to collapsing infrastructure. By 1968, most of the bridges needed substantial repair, and the following year, the line was very nearly dismantled and rebuilt in Devon on the trackbed of British Rail's Kingswear branch. Fortunately this fell through, as did various proposals to single the main line from Hythe to New Romney, and close the Dungeness 'branch' in its entirety.

The closures and cut-backs were somewhat masked by a rash of new lines, almost all built to the narrower gauge of 7¼ inches, and mostly on very different sites to the railways of the 1940s and 1950s. With the British seaside holiday seemingly on its last legs, and vandalism an increasing menace on public esplanades and parks, a new breed of entrepreneurs were seeking leases in country parks, either privately or local-authority owned, and increasingly in the grounds of an entirely new phenomenon: the garden centre.

Market gardens and nurseries had been around for decades, but some were being shaken up and commercialised, and new ones built, with cafés and entertainments, making them leisure destinations in their own right. For the aspirational young family of the 1980s, Sunday meant a trip to the garden centre for a meat pie, a few garden shrubs, and rides for the children. The garden centres were offering surplus land, security, a near 12-month busy season and a friendly welcome.

For the next quarter of a century, garden centres would become home to the majority of new railways, and some

The South Downs Light Railway was one of many successful collaborations between railway clubs and garden centres. Freelance 0-4-2 *Peggy* was built by the Exmoor Steam Railway, which produces a range of attractive, efficient and ruggedly commercial locos.

long-established railways and model engineering clubs were shutting up shop in urban and seaside parks to join the gold-rush. Nearly all of the new railways were 7¼-inch gauge, and mostly pretty formulaic, but some site managers saw the added value that came with a more impressive visitor attraction, and some fine examples were built.

PARKS REBORN

The twenty-first century saw a resurgence of interest in Britain's parks and open spaces, often bequeathed by Victorian philanthropists and now sadly neglected. But parks were right back at the heart of a new café culture – morning lattes around the WiFi hotspot, garlic panini and watercress soup for lunch, a healthy walk, and of course a ride on the Victorian steam railway that granddad had so enjoyed.

This turnaround was generally excellent news for the surviving miniature railways. Some iconic lines were revitalised alongside the parks they had served so long, with new permanent structures and steam back in a big way. And after half a century on the sidelines, the British seaside was making a comeback too. The traditional bucket-and-spade market was still there, but the middle classes were coming back in droves. Taking the air in the Victorian or Edwardian splendour of seaside towns like Scarborough and Hastings had become seriously *de rigueur*, and again, the railways that had made it through the lean years were to reap the rewards.

THE 2020s

Understanding this long history helps makes sense of the astonishing variety of miniature railways that have survived. There are obvious differences of scale, from machines that can be slung in the back of a hatchback to 2-ton monsters. And of design – from precisely engineered standard gauge models to the new 'minimal gauge': freestyle one-offs to no particular style or scale. Subtler differences reflect the era in which the

South Marine Park in South Shields has reinvented itself for the twenty-first century, with enhancements to the 9½-inch gauge Lakeshore Railway part of the scheme. *Nelly* is a rare visitor from the Brightwalton Light Railway.

railway was laid, then periodically rebuilt. In short, Britain's miniature railways have something for just about everyone.

The running speed and general thrill level of these lines can vary hugely. In Edwardian days some of the bigger railways thought nothing of public running at 20–30mph, and some of these lines have retained 'grandfather rights' to run – shall we say – faster than the average, often with cruder, open carriages. More modern examples, primarily those built since the genesis of Health and Safety culture in the 1970s, are more comfortable, but considerably slower, with lots of long-winded flag-waving, whistles and uniforms. Very small children and elderly grandparents will probably enjoy the kind that toddles around at walking pace, while youngsters and adventurous mums and dads might want a bit more excitement. Miniature railways *can* enthral the iPad generation, and your research starts here!

THE 5-INCH RAILWAY

A SCALE OF 1:12 equates more or less precisely to 4⅔-inch gauge, but it was from the slightly wider gauge of 4¾ inches that the smallest miniature railways would eventually evolve. They were big models though, and building, buying and transporting them in the late Victorian era was a hobby for the wealthiest gentlemen, although humbler engineers like Henry Greenly – best known for his impressive 15-inch gauge miniature locos – started with big models of this kind.

Despite 4⅔ inches being the 'correct' gauge, most engineers seem to have adopted 4¾ inches, but it's not precisely clear when and why 4¾ inches became 5 inches, the most likely reason being that it was exactly double the scale of the popular 2½-inch gauge, allowing plans to be scaled up or down with the minimum of fearsome mathematics! Whatever the reason, by the 1930s 5-inch gauge was becoming the standard, actively promoted by Greenly and others.

Even 7¼-inch gauge was considered a bit marginal for carrying passengers at the time, and that same reasoning would hold back the 5-inch for decades, although many raised tracks were built by engineering clubs and societies

The Mid-Land Railway at Barton House in Wroxton, Norfolk may be the only line in the world to run 3½-inch gauge locomotives and passenger stock. Note the guide wheels on the carriages.

The Strawberry Line at Keynsham is currently the only commercially run 5-inch gauge railway in the UK. It carried 70,000 passengers in its first year.

from the 1930s to the 1960s and some remain in use today. These are usually dual 5-/7¼-inch gauge, so on public running days, a train might combine a 5-inch locomotive with 7¼-inch passenger stock, which is arguably not a 5-inch miniature railway at all, and therefore cheating! A few club lines do carry passengers on 5-inch stock, and the raised track concept was used on the 3½-inch Mid-Land Railway at Barton House, Wroxham, Norfolk, which seems to be the smallest passenger-carrying railway in the UK. This 80-yard raised circuit was built in 1962 and both the locomotives and carriages are genuinely 3½-inch gauge, although the sit-astride carriages have rubber guide rollers at the bottom to ward off calamity. The line is private, but open to the public with the adjacent 7¼-inch Riverside Railway on an irregular basis.

Unlike 3½-inch gauge, 5-inch equipment can also be operated on conventional ground-level track, and club lines are increasingly being built this way, generally with dual 5-/7¼-inch gauge track, so passenger-carrying on the 5-inch rails is unusual. There is, however, a very select group of commercial 5-inch passenger-carrying lines, the first and best

The primary advantage of 5-inch gauge is that you can fit a great deal into a small space. The Strawberry Line not only has a long and complex track layout, but can boast an impressive Motive Power Depot!

known being the Strawberry Line, set up by railwayman Mike Bass in 1999 at the Avon Valley Country Park at Keynsham, between Bristol and Bath. This is a scale 5-inch gauge railway, with authentic wooden sleepers set in tiny 6mm ballast. As often happens, Mike bought the locomotive first (a 5-inch Maxitrak Warship), then built a passenger-carrying railway around it, against all advice. Fortunately, the gauge wasn't an issue, and the railway allegedly went on to carry 70,000 passengers in its first season, putting it among the busiest railways of this type anywhere.

The enterprise proved profitable enough for Mike to leave the 'big railway' in 2001 and concentrate on the Strawberry Line, to which he added some delightful attractions, including an indoor model railway and a working 5-inch gauge 'hump-shunting' yard. Mike retired in 2018, but the railway is still open, although without the extra attractions.

An extensive 5-inch gauge layout will fit in a modest space. The private Luscombe Valley Railway in Poole squeezes 850 feet of track into a plot measuring 100 × 67 feet.

There are probably only three other public lines: Riley's Miniature Railway next to the standard gauge Lavender Line at Isfield in East Sussex, and raised circuits at the Astley Green Colliery Museum in Lancashire, and Crampton Tower Museum, Broadstairs. But Riley's only opens intermittently for charity, and both the museum lines are currently out of use.

The special advantage of the gauge is the ease of lifting and transporting locomotives, and the ability to squeeze a complex layout into a small space. There are some impressive private lines of this kind, none of which are regularly open to the public, although a few hold open days, including the Luscombe Valley in Poole, the Blatchington Branch at Seaford near Brighton, and the Joys of Life near Bethesda in North Wales.

If you're looking for a main line to stretch the legs of your 5-inch gauge Pacific, the dual-gauge railway run by the East Somerset Society of Model & Experimental Engineers at the Bath & West Showground in Somerset is one of the best. This ½-mile line is primarily a 7¼-inch railway, open to the public during shows and exhibitions, but it's dual-gauge throughout, giving an impressive run for the little trains. Unfortunately, the 5-inch track is never open to the public.

7¼-INCH GAUGE

IN STARK CONTRAST to the 5-inch railways, 7¼-inch gauge has become the most successful format (the word 'scale' would be wrong here, as few locos are now of 'scale' size) both in the UK and worldwide, from Australia and New Zealand to Germany, the Netherlands and across North America, from New York to Hollywood. But to add a twist to an otherwise near-uniform picture, the more westerly US and Canadian states have generally adopted 7½-inch (apparently in error).

This success is not hard to explain. A 7¼-inch railway can be equipped with narrow gauge locomotives to haul large numbers of passengers, or with smaller near-scale locomotives and rolling stock for the purists. Or both.

Locomotives are widely available new or second-hand, gauge standards are long established and enforced (sometimes rather rigorously) by the 7¼-inch Gauge Society, and locomotives are easy to transport – at the small end of the scale at least. From being something of an oddity in the 1960s, there are now several hundred such railways open to the public in the UK, making it difficult to pick a representative selection.

The United States has some big layouts, to which nothing in the UK can compare, but there are several extensive railways here. It's hard to judge which of these is the biggest, as some figures are based on the length of track purchased (including sidings), while other railways give ride length, which might mean several circuits.

OPPOSITE
The Barnards Miniature Railway in Essex (see page 27) is one of the most interesting of the new 7¼-inch railways and home to an extensive fleet of locomotives, both diesel and steam.

GREAT COCKCROW, CHERTSEY

With a total of almost 2 miles of track, and a lot of history, the Great Cockcrow Railway must count among the finest of the 7¼-inch gauge lines. It dates back to 1946, when Sir John Samuel built the Greywood Central Railway around his house 'Greywood' near Walton-on-Thames. By 1962, Sir John and a group of volunteers had created a ¾-mile railway, fully signalled in keeping with standard gauge practice of the day, and even running timetabled trains. After Sir John's death in October 1964 the railway was saved by publisher Ian Allan, who purchased the whole thing and, with the assistance of the volunteers, moved it to its current site off Hardwick Lane near Chertsey.

The 7¼-inch gauge Great Cockcrow Railway has a fleet of fifty mostly pre-nationalisation steam locomotives, an impressive array of signals and nearly 2 miles of track.

Since the opening of the first short balloon loop in September 1968 the railway has expanded into a complex layout, encompassing some double-tracked main-line sections, a single-track branch of about 310 yards to Cockcrow Hill (added in 1979), the Jubilee Line (1997), and most recently, the Millennium Line, completed in 2000, which circles the branch.

To make life easier for visitors, trains generally follow 'Red' or 'Green' routes on running days, each giving a run of about 1¼ miles and a journey time of 15–20 minutes. The railway continues to grow, and the most recent development is a 'proper' station building at Hardwick Central, which opened in 2014.

As in the early Greywood days, the accent is on authenticity, and train movements are controlled by a range of signals, both semaphore and colour light, controlled from three

signalboxes using a variety of standard gauge power lever frames, track circuits, and an electric token system on single line sections.

The roster of up to fifty locomotives is predominantly 1:8 scale and largely composed of pre-nationalisation steam locomotives, mostly 4-6-0s, Atlantics and Pacifics, but with plenty of smaller machines too. Diesels used to be second-class citizens, relegated mainly to shunting duties, as on the Reverend Awdry's railway, but there are now two Westerns and *Teddy Bear*, a BR Class 14, all of which haul passenger trains. Most of the locomotives are owned by volunteers, although a small number were brought here from Greywood in the 1960s.

MOORS VALLEY, DORSET

Moors Valley is one of the most commercially impressive of the 7¼-inch gauge railways, having followed many others by migrating from an urban park to a local authority-run country park in 1985/86. The line is around 2,000 yards long, in the form of a 'stretched oval', a popular layout among the new breed of 7¼-inch lines, because it allows intensive operation, with the illusion of a double track section in the middle. At Moors Valley, the main station, Kingsmere is situated inside one end of this oval, the railway immediately entering a long double track section beside a lake. The track layout is a bit more complex at the other end, with the line performing a convoluted double loop around a play area, giving children several opportunities to pester for a ride! Operationally, this is quite a testing section, as it includes three tunnels, some sharp curves and

The 7¼-inch gauge Moors Valley Railway is the spiritual home of the Tinkerbell locomotive class. Three Tinkerbells pass during the railway's thirtieth anniversary celebrations in August 2016.

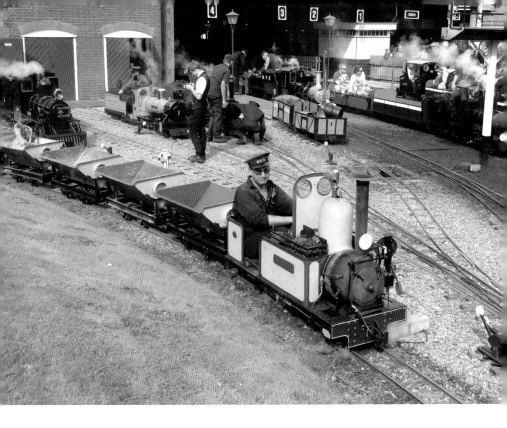

Kingsmere station on the Moors Valley Railway is a busy place during special events. The locomotive in the foreground is the original *Tinkerbell*.

steepish gradients. Lakeside, the intermediate station at the throat of this 'mountain' section is near the park entrance, so the railway arguably goes from A to B, rather than just providing leisure rides.

Returning to Kingsmere, the line runs back along the double section, through a fourth tunnel, and around a long, sharp curve giving views of the works and complex yard layout, before reappearing rather unexpectedly from the back wall of the Kingsmere terminus.

The workshops are always busy maintaining the railway's own locomotives and stock, as well as building new locomotives and overhauling older ones. The railway has become the actual and spiritual home of Roger Marsh's 'Tinkerbell' design, and numerous variants large and small have been produced there on Tinkerbell principles, both for the railway's own use and customers.

One of the charming elements of Moors Valley is its variety, from the tunnels, gradients and sinuous curves, to the lakeside vistas and busy yard and workshops. The proprietor, Jim Haylock has stuck loyally to aluminium rails over steel, a topic of some debate in the miniature railway world, as it results in frequent rail replacement, particularly on curves, but it gives a smoother, quieter ride and should be easier on wheelsets. Arguably, it also means that the track gets more regular inspection, which can only be a good thing.

Another unusual feature is that trains usually arrive at Kingsmere at one platform and are then hauled out and shunted back into the departures side for their next run. This sounds time-consuming, but it's a slick operation, giving visitors something to watch, and it simplifies pedestrian movements through the busy station.

BARNARDS MINIATURE RAILWAY

Several elaborate new-build railways have opened in the last few years, mostly to 7¼-inch gauge, and the Barnards Miniature Railway is one of the more interesting ones.

Just as the Faversham Miniature Railway has found a safe home at the National Fruit Tree Collection at Brogdale Farm, Faversham, Barnards winds through the National Malus Collection in Essex. Malus means apple, but these trees are breeding stock, so a pretty specialist attraction! This agricultural specialism fits well with a club-run miniature railway, as it's secure, spacious and generally allows enthusiasts to run trains more or less when they choose.

At Barnards, the railway has grown steadily, the first 280 yards from Burtonshaw terminus opening in 2010, then gradually extending to 1,300 yards in 2015, with completion to the buffer stops at the far terminus Angel Green, a total of 1,600 yards today. Burtonshaw has two platforms, with a third release road in the middle. The running line is single track – heading south, then west, skirting the end of a grass airstrip, to the two-platform Belvedere station, which forms the neck of a turn-back loop. Trains can either return here, or proceed in a northerly direction, around the other end of the airstrip to the passing loop and island platform at Sitooterie Halt (a third loop accesses a turntable), then turning east alongside the Fenchurch Street to Southend railway, to Angel Green, which has two platforms and a turntable. The two termini are thus quite close, the line having run more or less around the boundary of Barnards Farm.

The railway has a broad collection of locomotives, many from local company Mardyke, some rehomed from deceased miniature railways nearby. Thus Barnards might best be described as the home to the National Mardyke Collection! The first locomotive to arrive was a 1992 Mardyke Hymek, which arrived in 2010. It was later joined by two Mardyke Class 47s, one ex-Ness Island via Bolebroke Castle, and the other from Swanley New Barn. Centrepiece is the 1979 Mardyke Deltic *Royal Highland Fusilier*, which arrived in 2011, and was rebuilt the following year with two 6.5hp engines, an authentic touch, and claimed to be the only dual-engined miniature locomotive in the country. Another unusual machine is the 2-BEL two-car Pullman EMU *Barnards Belle*, based loosely on the Brighton Belle electric trains. The fleet of around ten steam locomotives encompasses just about everything, from a narrow-gauge 0-4-0 tank to a scale model of 2-10-0 British Rail Class 9F *Black Prince*.

BEAMISH COG RAILWAY

Rack railways – which gain traction and brake force by engaging a cog wheel on the locomotive with a set of raised teeth or 'rack' between the rails – are widely used in the Swiss Alps and a few other mountainous regions. Britain has two – the famous Snowdon Mountain Railway in North Wales, and the rather less well-known 7¼-inch gauge line operated by the Beamish Model Engineering Group (BMEG) at the

Living Museum of the North in County Durham. This includes a pretty conventional 280-yard circuit, plus one innocuous-looking siding that descends for 200 yards on a gradient as steep as 1:8 to a level section 50 feet below, using a Van Roll rack. This line came about because veteran club member Ken Swan had built a functioning

rack locomotive, 0-4-0RT *Koppel*, and wanted a rack railway to run it on. Most of the rack section is on a high viaduct, also designed by Ken, and built using steel blagged from British Steel. The viaduct is 100 feet long and up to 12 feet high – one of the biggest structures on any 7¼-inch miniature railway in the world, beaten only by the 216-foot O'Brien-Moore bridge in Los Angeles, but that is part clear span, and part wooden trestle.

There are only a handful of miniature rack railways in the world, including this 7¼-inch line operated by the Beamish Model Engineering Group.

Sadly, Health and Safety rules eventually caught up with the Beamish rack railway, and although it's still very much in operation, it no longer carries members of the public. Even before the ban, getting a ride could take some patience, because Ken's little Orenstein & Koppel locomotive could only handle a single carriage and up to four children or three adults on the climb. Nevertheless, the line often carried fifty to eighty passengers on an operating day.

Some thirty similar locomotives have now been built worldwide from Ken's plans, and some of these have visited the railway. Another club member built *Krokodil*, a battery-electric based loosely on the famous Swiss electric locomotive class, but this proved a technical failure.

The Beamish group has since built a petrol-hydraulic rack locomotive, a second rack-equipped Orenstein & Koppel, and

The 7¼-inch gauge Beer Heights Light Railway is a finely crafted and meticulously maintained line at the Peco model railway factory in Beer, Devon.

an 'adhesion-only' variant for use on the conventional railway. The rack, the locomotive class and the extraordinary viaduct all survive as a tribute to Ken Swan, a great engineer, who died in October 2018, aged 89.

BEER HEIGHTS

The Beer Heights Light Railway is at the other end of the country, near Seaton in Devon. In 1970 the Pritchard Patent Product company (PPP) – best known for Peco model railway equipment – moved to a larger factory in Beer, and added a shop and other visitor attractions, including a 7¼-inch miniature railway. This opened in 1975, and gradually grew to its current length of about a mile in 1989. As a manufacturer of quality model railway equipment, PPP wanted the railway to showcase its engineering strengths, and the Beer Heights is maintained to the highest standards. Crammed onto a constricted and steeply sloping site above the factory, the railway has plenty of gradients, curves and structures, offering sea views and other unexpected vistas. Day-to-day operations are typically flawless, with plenty on offer for visitors young and old, from the immaculate locomotives and smart efficient staff, to technical details like the real-time track circuit diagram.

The railway features what is thought to be the deepest cutting on any 7¼-inch gauge railway (25 feet), and a long S-shaped tunnel under the car park that must break some sort of record. It's certainly the darkest of its kind. Track is single throughout, but careful planning gives the impression that you're setting out on a four-track main line, then experiencing the charms of a rural branch.

The railway runs from Easter to late October and in peak periods is operated with two trains and three locomotives, one being turned, watered and fettled between turns, while the other two are out on the circuit, which is fully signalled. At quiet times, a single diesel train may suffice, but on special running days, the automatic signalling allows numerous trains to run at once.

David Curwen's 0-4-2 *Dickie* is on the first circuit of 'Mount Delight' on the Beer Heights Light Railway, with the sea just visible 300 feet below. In a few minutes the train will return and enter the tunnel beneath the photographer.

8-INCH TO 12-INCH GAUGE

BANKSIDE MINIATURE RAILWAY

A very small number of railways were built to unusual gauges, generally because someone had fallen in love with a locomotive and built a railway around it. This applied with the 9-inch gauge Faversham Railway in Kent, and the handful of 9½-inch lines: Lakeshore Railroad in South Shields, Hall Leys at Matlock, and Downs School near Malvern. There is at least some historic precedent with these lines, as both gauges equate closely to 1:6 scale, so a few were built, but there is no such excuse for the 8¼-inch Bankside Railway at Eastleigh, for which there seems to be no precedent, and no one knows why the unknown engineer chose to build a raised track to this peculiar gauge.

The Bankside Railway is unique in almost every respect. *Carolyn* waits for passengers at the terminus.

The gauge was chosen by an employee of a traction engine manufacturer who built the attractive tank locomotive *Carolyn* in 1924. With her unique raised track and sit-astride carriages, *Carolyn* led a peripatetic life, running at fairs and shows for many years, but largely staying out of the enthusiast's gaze, until she was bought by Bert Merritt of Eastleigh in the 1960s and run by him at a few locations until he made a permanent track at the Brambridge Park Garden Centre near his home in 1977.

Because of the lack of points at Bankside, the easiest way to run round is to turn the whole train on this giant 35-foot turntable.

The railway started out as a 110-yard out-and-back, but the Merritt family extended this into a balloon loop in 2001. Because conventional points are tricky to engineer with sit-astride carriages, the railway chose an unusual arrangement at the 'neck' of the loop. Trains depart across a turntable from one of two platforms, and while out on the track, an assistant moves the turntable round to the return track, sending the whole train across the turntable to the arrivals platform. Running around would be complicated if the turntable were not 35 feet long, enabling the loco and up to four carriages to be backed out and turned, then put back into the departure side, a slick operation that brings the operational bonus of separating arriving and departing passengers. All approaches to the turntable are protected by colour light signals indicating that the table is correctly set and locked.

The railway is 500 yards long, and features a 1:60 climb in the anti-clockwise direction, steepening briefly to 1:35 near the only wayside station, Falconhigh Halt. This is all a bit much for a unique 96-year-old locomotive, so the family team (Bert died a few years back, leaving his son Peter to run the line, with *his* son Simon assisting) is building the world's second 8¼-inch gauge loco, a 2-6-0 tank to be named *H G Merritt* in Bert's memory. Hopefully, the new loco will be in service for *Carolyn*'s centenary in 2024.

WELLS & WALSINGHAM

From the unique and small to the unique and very large, the Wells & Walsingham Light Railway in Norfolk claims to be the longest (surviving) 10¼-inch gauge railway in the world, almost certainly the longest ever built, and the smallest public railway, as it was constructed – and continues to operate – under a Light Railway Order. It runs for 4 miles from the seaside town of Wells-next-the-Sea inland to the village of Little Walsingham, which has been a place of worship and pilgrimage for almost a thousand years.

Cdr Francis exchanges a few words with the driver of *Norfolk Heroine* at Wells in 2012. She is undoubtably one of the most impressive 10¼-inch gauge locomotives ever made.

The railway runs on the trackbed of the former Great Eastern's Wells branch line, which succumbed in the Beeching era. The audacious scheme to rebuild part of it was the work of one man, ex-Royal Naval officer, Commander Roy Francis. After his retirement in 1957, Francis decided to turn his garden railway hobby into a business, first with a portable 10¼-inch gauge line, then by establishing the (relatively) modest 1,200-yard Wells Harbour Railway in 1976, which served the dual purpose of carrying tourists from the town to the sand dunes, and residents of a seaside caravan park into the town.

Norfolk Heroine tackles the climb out of Wells at the start of the longest 10¼-inch railway in the world. The train has another 4 miles to run.

Construction of the bigger and bolder line to Walsingham began in 1979, although the application to reopen the level-crossing over the A149 was refused, forcing the Wells terminus to the edge of the town, rather than the old station, or even a connection with the Harbour line.

Completed in 1982, the gradients and heavy traffic soon overwhelmed the line's little 0-6-0 tank loco *Pilgrim*. Nothing on the second-hand market seemed able to offer the range and endurance required to haul heavy trains for 4 miles, so Commander Francis came up with another audacious plan to build something suitable, and with the backing of patron the Earl of Leicester, who had been brought up in Zimbabwe, an African-style 2-6-0 + 0-6-2 Garratt was commissioned, and completed in 1986. Named in honour of one-time Norfolk resident Admiral Lord Nelson, *Norfolk Hero* had tractive effort of 1,400lb and could carry up to 146 gallons of water – more than enough to haul trains of up to a hundred passengers out to Walsingham. So successful was the locomotive, it was joined in 2011 by a similar machine named *Norfolk Heroine* in honour of local nurse Edith Cavell, who had helped allied prisoners escape during the First World War and was controversially executed by the Germans in 1915.

Norfolk Heroine entered service as the fourth locomotive on the railway, the other two being diesels, both pretty powerful in 10¼-inch terms, but not a patch on the big Garratts. The line can be tricky to work, because the gradient chart is something of a switchback, with a long 1:80 climb out of Wells under trees that often leave the rails wet and greasy, followed by a series of peaks and troughs, some as steep as 1:60, and a final climb into Walsingham at 1:80. This was much steeper in the early days until a cutting was dug out, restoring the original profile.

The railway typically runs from the beginning of March to the end of October. As a rule, only one engine will be out on the line at a time, as there is no passing loop and with a running time of about 30 minutes each way, trains are able to complete an out-and-back turn in about an hour and a half.

EASTLEIGH LAKESIDE RAILWAY

The Eastleigh Lakeside Steam Railway has virtually no history in itself, as the line only opened on temporary track in 1992, and it was not until 1998 that Eastleigh Borough Council finally relented and granted a sufficiently long lease for construction of the full 1¼-mile railway and Parkway station, a few minutes' walk from Southampton Airport Parkway station. These major works were completed in 2000, with the tunnel (long enough for your eyes to get acclimatised!) following in 2003, and the café and toilet facilities in 2005.

Eastleigh Lakeside is dual 10¼-inch and 7¼-inch gauge, but the third 7¼-inch rail is primarily used by visiting locos. The line has a waisted circuit form, with a particularly long double track section in the middle. Signalling is mostly automatic, controlled by track circuit, with colour light signals on block sections, and an impressive array of pneumatic semaphores controlling movements in the station departure area.

Trains depart from Parkway running anti-clockwise, through what can for once justifiably be called a station 'throat', to the right-hand running line, climbing on quite a stiff gradient. After crossing a footpath and curving to the left, the return track gradually pulls away on a lower level, as our line continues to climb, breasting the summit more or less on a level with the roof of the tunnel. From here there's a gradual descent to Monks Brook Halt.

Monks Brook is on a sharp loop, with three crossings and a steep gradient under trees, but soon back in the open, coasting down through the 100-yard tunnel. A gentle climb brings the line up to the outward track, followed by a long coast back to take the right-hand road onto the bottom loop, ending in a sharp curve up into Parkway. This is a steep climb, with the home signal for the platform just before the top.

An impressive line-up of 7¼-inch and 10¼-inch locos at Eastleigh's steam depot in 2011. The number varies, but the railway usually has fifteen or more steam locos rostered to the shed.

Eastleigh Lakeside's Parkway station has all the atmosphere of a big terminus. H.C.S. Bullock's 1002 *The Empress* (right) is about to depart, with Alfred Doves' *Coronation* just visible on a shed road behind.

Stopping here can be fatal with a heavy train, so experienced drivers hang back in the valley to get a good fire and a clear run at the summit.

When the country park was new, the landscape was a bit barren, but it looks better now, with mature trees and shrubs and diverse flora and fauna. The railway has become part of this 're-wilding', and it's fortunate to have got in early, as it probably couldn't be built or significantly altered here today.

The railway is a worthy successor to the legendary Surrey Border & Camberley and gives SB&CR locomotives a chance to stretch their legs, as their designer H.C.S. Bullock intended. Eastleigh has around twenty steam locomotives, and a couple of diesels, and although it doesn't own all of Bullock's locomotives, it has acquired most of them, and been instrumental in retrieving and restoring many others. The railway has one of the most impressive workshops of any miniature line, with work divided between regular servicing of the day-to-day passenger stock and locomotives, restoration of twentieth-century machines by Bullock and others, and the occasional new build.

Owners of other iconic machinery (notably Kerr's of Arbroath) often send locomotives down for special events, bringing together whole fleets once scattered far and wide. The railway is, in effect, a working museum, and a fitting tribute to Britain's engineering tradition, and to Bullock in particular – a genius in many ways, who is only today getting the respect he deserves. With the nearby Eastleigh railway works being run down, the miniature railway proudly upholds a 130-year tradition of railway engineering in the town.

HASTINGS MINIATURE RAILWAY

There are few remaining 10¼-inch gauge seaside railways, and the Hastings Miniature Railway is probably the only survivor that actually runs on the beach. Like many others, it has experienced wild swings in popularity and investment over the decades, but it's one of the lucky ones, emerging into the new millennium as a vibrant and successful local business. The line was initially put down on the beach at neighbouring St Leonards in 1947 by Captain Howey of Romney, Hythe

A classic scene at Rock-a-Nore, with net-drying huts and cliff railway behind. *Uncle Jim* was built for the railway in 1968 by operator J. Hughes and was subsequently named in his memory.

Marine Parade station in Hastings, with *Edmund Hannay* in the platform. Hannay was built for the Wells Harbour Railway, arriving at Hastings in 2015.

& Dymchurch fame, then moved to Hastings old town and sold to a consortium including railway publisher Ian Allan.

Originally very short, the railway was extended in the 1950s and is now around half a mile in length, linking the fishermen's 'village' at Rock-a-Nore, with its iconic net-drying huts, westwards to the brash lights and amusements of the Marine Parade. Rock-a-Nore station has changed a great deal over the years, from a single platform, to twin platforms with a turntable in the hectic days of the 1950s, back to a basic single-platform halt in the belt-tightening diesel days of the 1980s, and with the turntable restored in 2011. The carriage sheds are located here, plus a busy workshop from 2011 because – like Eastleigh – the Hastings line undertakes all sorts of engineering work. The single line runs westwards to East Beach Street station, which has evolved in a similar way to Rock-a-Nore. Originally the westerly terminus, it became a passing loop with an island platform in 1959 when the line was extended, then closed together with the loop in the 1980s. The loop and a single platform were restored in 2010 to allow two-train running. Marine Parade station, the other terminus, has a single platform, a large station building and a run-round loop.

Initially operated by Bullock 0-6-0 pannier-tank *Firefly* (since rebuilt as a tender locomotive) and a 1938 Bassett-Lowke

Royal Scot, the railway was 'diesel-ised' in 1984, in line with the general rationalisation of the period. As part of the restoration of the line, steam returned in 2015, and Hastings is today home to an eclectic mix of diesel, steam and steam-outline locomotives. As at Kerr's, the railway has located, bought and restored several locomotives that ran here in the past, and other locos – both Hastings old-timers and strangers – pay regular visits. With occasional test-runs by new or refurbished locos from the 'works' as well, it is an interesting place for the enthusiast.

In 2015, the railway took control of the 7¼-inch gauge Alexandra Park Miniature Railway on the other side of Hastings, some three-quarters of a mile inland from the beach. The first railway at Alexandra Park was built in 1970 near the boating lake, but only lasted a couple of years. In 1982 the East Sussex Model Engineers moved its operations from Collinswood Drive, St Leonards, and built a 130-yard 3½-inch, 5-inch and 7¼-inch gauge circuit at the top end of Alexandra Park. This eventually fell into disuse and was rebuilt in the winter of 2015/16 as a 250-yard 7¼-inch line, known – slightly confusingly – as the Hastings Miniature Railway Alexandra Park (don't get directions to the wrong one!). Another offshoot of Hastings' historic seafront line is RVM Engineering, the company's engineering arm, which is based at Rock-a-Nore. RVM maintains the rolling stock for both railways, and does much freelance manufacturing and restoration work for other 7¼-inch and 10¼-inch railways as well.

Automatic crossings are unusual on 10¼-inch railways. No.24 Sandy River approaches the Riverside terminus at Trago Mills in 2008.

BICKINGTON STEAM RAILWAY

Trago Mills operates four out-of-town retail and garden centres. One of these, at Newton Abbot in Devon,

Alice – seen here arriving at Trago Central – came from Kessingland with Brian Nicholson.

is home to the Bickington Steam Railway, one of the most interesting modern 10¼-inch gauge railways, and well worth a visit, even if you don't have any shopping to do. In 1987, Trago Mills' boss, Mike Robertson, let the franchise to build and operate a miniature railway at the Newton Abbot store to former headmaster Brian Nicholson and his son David, who had just received a surprise rent increase for their existing 10¼-inch line at Kessingland Wildlife Park near Lowestoft.

Trago Mills landscaped a former quarry at the Newton Abbot site, to include the railway, a boating lake and other amenities, and – remarkable though it sounds today – the long and complex railway was finished in five months, opening in May 1988.

The story goes that the Nicholsons told Trago Mills to allow for a *maximum* permissible gradient of 1:50, with a sharpest permissible curve of 50-foot radius, and somewhere down the chain these figures were adopted as the working norm!

Sharp curves and gradients as steep as 1:40 are everywhere at Trago Mills, making it particularly challenging for drivers and an entertaining ride for passengers. The line begins at the three-platform Riverside terminus in the car park near the store entrance, and forms a balloon loop. In practice, with two smaller loops on the big one, the layout is hard to follow, even after several rides. Earthworks are quite impressive in places, and there are three tunnels and a major viaduct too.

The line runs via Goose Glen Halt, a lakeside station convenient for the other amusements, to the two-platform Trago Central station at the back of the store near the garden centre, which is actually closer on foot from Riverside, but the line can still be useful for carrying big purchases back to the car park.

The locomotive fleet has waxed and waned over the years, but still includes three of the machines that arrived here from Kessingland: David Curwen's 4-4-2 *Blanche of Lancaster*, 2-6-4T *E R Calthrop* and 2-6-0 *Alice*. Two more recent additions are *D5910*, a Class 23 'Baby Deltic' diesel-hydraulic built by David in the railway's own workshop in 1987, and 2-6-2 *Sandy River*, a narrow-gauge machine, built by Colby-Simkins in 1991, and based on the 2-foot gauge steam locomotives of the Sandy River & Rangeley Lakes Railroad. These have become popular prototypes for miniature locomotives, because they are big machines – effectively 1:2¼ scale on 10¼-inch gauge. *Sandy River* was built for Trago's new Merthyr Tydfil store, then under construction, but the leisure park remains on hold, and *Sandy River* has become a mainstay of operations at Newton Abbot.

Ride-in miniature diesel locomotives are not always successful designs, but *D5910*, designed and built by railway owner David Nicholson, is one of the best. In 1993 it arrives at Trago Central.

12¼-INCH TO 15-INCH GAUGE

ONE OF THE rarest miniature gauges is 12¼-inch, which has origins in a handful of early twentieth-century 12-inch lines: Chessington Zoo (1932), Paignton Zoo (1937), and Ruislip Lido (1945). Ruislip Lido was built to suit the 12-inch 4-4-2 *Prince Edward*, and three years later Littlehampton was built for existing 12¼-inch locomotives. Even in the 1980s neither was clearly dominant, with Fairbourne (15-inch converted to 12¼-inch in 1986) and Bognor, which was re-gauged from 10¼-inch to 12-inch in 1987, but that would be the last 12-inch railway. Buxton was re-gauged from 10¼-inch to 12¼-inch in 1998, Exbury Gardens a new build at 12¼-inch in 2001, and Poole is now in the process of conversion from 10¼-inch to 12¼-inch.

It might be rare now, but 12¼-inch has real future potential, because to be frank, passengers are getting bigger and heavier! On a 12¼-inch line, locos can be built to the sort of scale and power you might expect to find on a 15-inch gauge railway, with carriages offering similar seating capacity. But the equipment is cheaper, curves can be sharper, and operations simpler, as it comes in below the 350mm (13¾-inch) lower limit for the Railway Inspectorate to become involved.

Being a new standard, there are few historic machines around, although the Fairbourne has a few, and the railway commissioned by Leo de Rothschild at Exbury Gardens, with its Exmoor Steam locomotives and immaculate infrastructure and buildings, is undoubtably a classic of the future.

OPPOSITE
The 2013 fire (see page 53) demonstrated the Ravenglass & Eskdale's vulnerability to a shortage of locomotives, and after a global search, the railway settled on *Pinta*, built by German manufacturer Krauss in 1929. Renamed *Whillan Beck* in early 2018, in November 2017 it is prepared for a commissioning run.

Naomi being turned at Exbury. Every element of the railway is maintained in immaculate condition, from the starched uniforms to the locomotives and even the buildings.

Of the others, Ruislip Lido – the last surviving 12-inch line – is probably the most interesting. The railway was originally built in the form of a 1,000-yard circuit based around Woody Bay station on the quieter northeast side of the Ruislip Lido in north London. If the place sounds like a bathing pool, that's only partially true, because it's actually a

The Rock Garden at Exbury is one of the biggest in Europe, and the railway fits the landscape to perfection.

reservoir built in 1811 to supply the nearby Grand Junction Canal and transport water to London. It became a popular spot for visitors, and enhancements gradually began to appear, including the Lido Health Spa in 1936, an artificial beach, and the railway in 1945.

The line led a quiet life until a serious derailment in 1978 led to closure. But the council invested in safety improvements and put out a call for volunteers to run the line, resulting in the formation of the Ruislip Lido Railway Society, which took over in 1980. The Society has extended the railway by eliminating the return loop and extending the double track north, then west around the Lido, where it reduces to a single line, through a passing loop at Haste Hill station, then back to single track to the big new terminus at Willow Lawn, near the Lido entrance. The total *track* length is almost 2½ miles, claimed as the longest 12-inch line in the country. Surely the Fairbourne in Wales is longer? It is, but cheekily Ruislip is talking about 12-inch gauge, although gauge widening on curves certainly takes it into 12¼-inch territory in places.

An immaculate and fascinating collection of rolling stock on the Ruislip Lido railway, from the veteran scale model Western to a good selection of practical modern equipment based on 15-inch and 2-foot gauge practice. Such is the flexibility of 12¼-inch gauge!

The Ruislip Lido has something for everyone: an attractive woodland and lakeside setting, a selection of interesting locomotives, and a varied and fascinating history. Arguably the most interesting locomotive is *Mad Bess*, built over twelve years by the Ruislip Lido Railway Society and finally completed in 1998, bristling with modern technology.

Most stock is thought to be transferable between the Lido and the nominally 12¼-inch railways, and attempts are finally being made to establish common standards.

Rolling stock is a mixed bag. *Prince Edward* was sold in 1959 and is now in private hands, although it makes occasional visits to Ruislip during special events. It was replaced by a petrol-electric US-style loco that ran until 1973, when it too was replaced by petrol-hydraulic Western *Robert*, built by Severn Lamb in 1973 to broadly the same design and layout as David Curwen's exquisite machines, but not quite cracking the Western style in the same way. The locomotive did well mechanically though, and is still in use after 47 years.

Robert was joined in 1998 by the magnificent *Mad Bess. Bess* is based on the Ffestiniog's Hunslet *Blanche* and is technically a 2-4-0ST+T. In other words, it has a saddle tank, and a separate tender (tank behind). The loco was built at the railway over twelve years, and it's interesting for all sorts of reasons, not least being the design criterion to be

A clash of scales, but who cares? Severn Lamb Western *Robert* leads *Mad Bess* hauling a special train to mark the fortieth year of the Railway Society.

River Irt is technically the oldest working 15-inch gauge locomotive in the world; it started life as Sir Arthur Heywood's *Muriel* in 1894 but has been much rebuilt over the last century. Having left 'The Green', the train is just starting a short 1:35 climb: one of the steepest gradients used by any passenger service in the UK.

easily re-gaugable to 15-inch should that ever be required, and oil-firing to protect the woods around the Lido from glowing embers.

Bread-and-butter traction is provided by the Ravenglass-built No.5 *Lady of the Lakes* (1986), and three similar and eminently sensible diesels built by Severn Lamb: No.7 *Graham Alexander* (1990), No.8 *Bayhurst* (2003) and No.9 *John Rennie* (2004).

RAVENGLASS & ESKDALE

Like the Romney, the Ravenglass & Eskdale Railway (R&ER) in Cumbria is 15-inch gauge and a world-famous heritage railway. Both have survived for almost a century, but their

The Ravenglass & Eskdale was originally a ramshackle 3-foot gauge mineral line. Adventurous Edwardian tourists soon discovered its charms, but the passenger service died in 1908 when the Board of Trade demanded improvements.

characters are subtly different, the Ravenglass being a tad more raffish, with a younger feel, although it's actually much older.

The railway started life in 1875 as a 3-foot gauge mineral line, built to bring iron ore down from Eskdale to the Furness Railway's main line at Ravenglass. Passenger services were very much an afterthought in this sparsely populated country, but a service of sorts commenced in 1876 only to be withdrawn in 1908 when the Board of Trade demanded improvements, and the company decided it wasn't worth the effort, despite early stirrings of tourist traffic. By 1913, even the iron ore trade had melted away, and the line was closed in its entirety.

Meanwhile, the firm of Bassett-Lowke, through its offshoot Narrow Gauge Railways Ltd, was busy establishing miniature railways and looking for a site to build and operate a big 15-inch gauge line, partly through the sheer enthusiasm of W.J. Bassett-Lowke and others, but also to provide a testbed for locomotives, 'proof of concept' for customers and hopefully return an operating profit too. The company organised a site visit to Ravenglass early in 1915, signed a lease, and rapidly re-gauged the first mile out from Ravenglass station, with the first tourist services running later in the summer. Despite the war – which had yet to develop into a grim fight to the death – conversion work continued, and by Easter 1917, the entire 7 miles to Dalegarth, deep in the Fells, was open.

The line was an immediate success, and locomotives and rolling stock were scraped together from wherever they could be found, resulting in an eclectic mix of 'minimum gauge' equipment from Sir Arthur Heywood's stable and scale miniatures from Bassett-Lowke, including Atlantic *Sans Pareil*, and Henry Greenly's showpiece *John Anthony*, the first 15-inch gauge Pacific (indeed, the second Pacific of any kind in Britain). This imposing machine was built to the order of J.E.P. (later Captain) Howey for his garden railway, but Howey's mind was already on much bigger things, and it was

Northern Rock looks old, but it actually entered service in 1976, with many features borrowed from best practice over the preceding century. It has proved very reliable in service, and is one of the most powerful 15-inch locomotives in the world.

bought by the R&ER, where it was renamed *Colossus*. Soon afterwards, a collision between these two miniature locos resulted in the company purchasing *Ella* and *Muriel* from the estate of Sir Arthur Heywood, who had recently died. In 1922, the railway established a granite quarry at Beckfoot to keep the line busy in the harsh winter months, and summer tourist traffic continued to expand.

The passenger trains were withdrawn in the Second World War, but granite traffic kept the line ticking along. After the war, the railway was acquired by the Keswick Granite Company, owners of the Beckfoot quarry, but the quarry closed in 1953, and by 1960, the company was preparing to abandon the little railway on just about any terms, with wholesale scrappage the most likely fate.

Luckily for us all, a preservation society was rapidly formed and the railway was saved. Over the following decades, the railway company and the society gradually renovated and improved the line, with the now-familiar mix of volunteer, full-time and part-time labour. There isn't room here to touch on the complex building and rebuilding of locomotives both before and after preservation, but the steam fleet was later supplemented by new build No.10 *Northern Rock*, a 2-6-2 built in the railway's own workshops at Ravenglass in 1976.

Douglas Ferreira is the workhorse of the R&ER: popular with drivers, and always ready to haul anything, night and day, in all weathers. In October 2014, it tackles the steep climb out of Beckfoot with the first train of the day.

The following year, *Silver Jubilee* entered service – a three-car diesel multiple unit of the kind common on the standard gauge, but unusual in the miniature world. At the time the railway was having some success running early and late 'social' services and even a school train, for which *Silver Jubilee* was well suited. When these ceased in 2001,

the machine's *raison d'être* was gone, and it was eventually turned into normal passenger stock.

The R&ER's mixed bag of historic rail-tractors and other odd machinery has been joined by two big diesels: *Lady Wakefield* was built at Ravenglass in 1980 and is a typical Bo-Bo diesel-hydraulic, with a 112hp Perkins engine; *Douglas Ferreira* was commissioned by the preservation society from TMA Engineering in Birmingham in 2005. Designed using best practice from *Lady Wakefield*, and diesel experience from the Romney, Hythe & Dymchurch, this Bo-Bo locomotive had a 125hp Perkins diesel, hydraulic transmission and two spacious cabs, giving excellent visibility. Since entering service in 2006, the locomotive has become the mainstay of the fleet and arguably one of the most successful miniature diesels ever made.

This workhorse really came into its own when a series of workshop fires in late 2012 and 2013 put most of the railway's

Douglas Ferreira catches the morning sun as it crosses the Ravenglass road on an early passenger turn.

The original Ravenglass & Eskdale museum opened at Ravenglass in 1978, but was rehoused in a new building in 2017, with funding from a variety of sources. The loco in the foreground has been rebuilt around the remaining fragments of *Katie*, Sir Arthur Heywood's pioneering minimum gauge locomotive of 1896.

locomotives out of action, and *Douglas Ferreira* shouldered much of the workload for months on end. The diesel was itself damaged after running low on oil in April 2013, but was quickly re-engined and back at work.

The fires made it all too apparent that the R&ER was short of front-line steam, which was solved with the purchase of the 1929-vintage Pacific *Pinta*, built by German manufacturer Krauss for the 1929 Ibero-American Exposition in Spain. After considerable recommissioning work, she was re-christened *Whillan Beck* (all front-line R&ER locos are named after local rivers) in Ravenglass early in 2018 and has proved a star performer, adding a shade of the exotic to the railway's very British fleet.

The Ravenglass & Eskdale Railway is steeped in history, and rightly celebrated as the spiritual home of the whole miniature railway concept. Long may it uphold that fine tradition!

ROMNEY, HYTHE & DYMCHURCH

The 15-inch gauge RH&D is probably better known and recorded than any other miniature railway in the world. In nearly a century, it has seen hugely profitable years and long lean decades, 'real' public service trains, a world war in which it played an active role, near bankruptcy and several 'grown up' tragedies, but it thrives today as a big local employer, and a centrepiece of the Romney Marsh tourist industry. The railway has almost everything, from a fleet of priceless iconic locomotives, a genuinely double-track main line, and busy stations in a string of small towns, yet it is still a miniature railway, although bound by the safety strictures of the big railway.

The line was the brainchild of two 1920s playboys, J.E.P. Howey, heir to a huge Australian fortune, and Count Louis Zborowski. The pair were passionate racing drivers, but once hooked by the might and grace of miniature steam locomotives (Howey is supposed to have detected the waft of steam and followed his nose to H.C.S. Bullock's workshop), it was inevitable that they would purchase locomotives of their own, and create a race track of a line to run them on.

In June 2017, the Romney, Hythe & Dymchurch Railway celebrated its ninetieth anniversary with a series of events. Here *Typhoon* crosses Collins Bridge, with the Collins Express. With a span of 60 feet, this is the longest underbridge on the railway.

The project very nearly died. First they failed to purchase the Ravenglass & Eskdale, then Zborowski was killed in the 1924 Monaco Grand Prix, but Howey decided to carry on alone, and after scouring the kingdom for a suitable railway to adapt, Howey ended up on the Romney Marshes in Kent, an area poorly served by rail for historical reasons.

The local community was by no means 100 per cent behind the project, which was seen – rightly enough – as a playboy scheme, and too small to be of much benefit to local people, who were quite well served by buses. Nevertheless, a Light Railway Order was granted in 1926, and Henry Greenly commissioned to design a fleet of locomotives, mostly ordered from Davey Paxman of Colchester, where two had already been built on Zborowski's order.

The double-track line opened in July 1927 from Hythe to New Romney, via railway-less Dymchurch, a distance of about 8 miles. It proved a winner that first year, encouraging Howey to seek permission for an extension to the wild end of the marshes at Dungeness, setting about construction even before the Light Railway Order was amended. This single-track 'branch line', with a terminal loop near Dungeness lighthouse, opened in August 1928, creating an unbroken 14-mile ribbon of steel – a fair length for a standard gauge branch, let alone a 15-inch railway.

The line flourished, and continued to carry locals and tourists into the early days of the Second World War, but it was soon requisitioned to carry troops to remote camps on the marshes, and the military even introduced an armoured train to provide a mobile anti-aircraft battery, and take a last desperate stand, should Hitler's troops land on the beach. Luckily it never came to that, but the railway played a crucial PR role, by keeping spirits up on the Home Front and demonstrating to the world (and Mr Hitler, of course) that if Britain was armouring its toy trains it really was serious about fighting on.

Like most British railways, the line was left in an appalling state when hostilities ceased, but Howey regained control in July 1945 and set about rebuilding the railway, a process that took two years of toil and tears just to get the infrastructure sorted, with locomotive and rolling stock issues dragging on for decades. Fortunately, this expensive and time-consuming operation proved worthwhile, because the post-war years saw good business, although Howey's death in 1963 resulted in the sale of the line in 1964. Four years later it was sold again, by which time the wear and tear of those busy years and general lack of investment had taken a toll on bridges and other structures the length of the line.

The late 1960s and early 1970s were a time of general retrenchment, particularly on a small railway saddled with

It's no surprise that a double track miniature railway designed by a pair of playboy motor-racing drivers would be designed for speed. In 2016, *Winston Churchill* approaches Dymchurch, between Hythe and New Romney.

big expenses, but the railway survived outright closure, and the sort of desperate measures British Rail was adopting to keep track on the ground. From these miserable years, the fight back was to be a long haul, punctuated by some heart-breaking level-crossing collisions, and a remorseless decline in passenger numbers that forced the railway to go cap in hand for grants and public money wherever it could be found. There were high-spots, however, such as the innovative daily school train that ran from 1977 until very recently.

Today, the Romney, Hythe & Dymchurch is one of the most important tourist destinations in the southeast of England. Money will always be tight, but today's railway is slickly managed and run with great dedication by a team of full-time staff, backed up by faithful volunteers. Its stable of 1930s steam locomotives are among the best-known miniature locomotives in the world, and are highly prized and maintained to big railway standards. A proper main line in miniature.

NORTH BAY, SCARBOROUGH

This is one of the most unusual miniature railways in the UK, and quite unlike any other, from the track gauge to the locomotives and even the layout. So it's rather fitting to give it the last word.

Scarborough's North Bay Railway is an end-to-end 20-inch gauge line of about 1,500 yards, built originally from a turning triangle at the southernmost station, Peasholm Park, to the northern terminus in the outlying village of Scalby Mills, where the loco (not the whole train, sadly!) was turned using an odd balloon loop laid partly underground in a cliff-face tunnel. The railway opened with that layout in 1931, but just a year later, the Peasholm triangle became a more conventional loop. Thirty years after that the tunnel started to collapse at Scalby Mills, so a turning triangle was

put in there instead, although by 1988 that too had been replaced with a turntable and run-round loop. For the public though, little has changed. The railway is a straightforward out-and-back line, with a passing loop half-way along at Beach station, although passengers do not usually board or alight here today.

The railway was intended to be a short 18-inch gauge circuit within the newly landscaped Peasholm Park, then a more conventional 15-inch gauge line out to Scalby Mills, which was about to be developed. For reasons unknown, the council finally chose the unusual gauge of 20 inches and steam-outline diesels. Hudswell Clarke – better known for its standard gauge steam engines – won the tender to supply three LNER-style 4-6-2 Pacifics. These were steam-outline diesels modelled on *Flying Scotsman*: *Neptune*, *Triton* and *Poseidon*, later joined by a chunkier 4-6-4T *Robin Hood*, which was actually built for a park railway in Leeds that failed.

In 2007, four of the original 20-inch gauge machines were brought together at North Bay (left to right): *Robin Hood*, *Triton*, *Neptune* and *Poseidon*. *Neptune* has run here since the railway opened in 1931, *Triton* arrived the following year, and the other two worked on a variety of railways before re-joining their classmates.

Robin Hood being turned at Scalby Mills. The train used to turn here using a rather exciting tunnel into the cliff, but when this began to fail, it was replaced with a turning 'Y', and later with a conventional turntable.

Determined to stay afloat in the Great Depression, Hudswell Clarke and Co. built nine similar locomotives in all, the others going to 21-inch gauge lines at Blackpool Pleasure Beach and various Butlins holiday camp railways. Their subsequent histories are rather complex, involving a tangle of name changes; nine survived, although one was a replacement for a machine destroyed by fire in Blackpool within the first year. Hudswell Clarke itself did less well, following standard gauge steam into oblivion, and of the 'broad gauge' miniature railways, only Scarborough and Blackpool saw in the new millennium. Nevertheless, four of the 20-inch locomotives still work at Scarborough, another three 21-inch machines are working at Blackpool, and two Princess Royal Class Pacifics built for Butlins have been preserved by the Princess Royal Locomotive Trust at Ripley in Derbyshire. Not a bad haul after 90-odd years.

FURTHER READING

Selected so as to give a broad scope, some of these books are historic titles, out of print today, but are fairly easy to find second-hand.

Allan, Ian. *ABC Miniature Railways*. Various publication dates. A to B Books, from 2006. (editor David Henshaw)

Buck, Stan. *Katie's Other Sisters: The 15" Gauge Locomotives of E. W. Twining & Trevor Guest*. Sian Project Group, 2007.

Bullock, Kenneth Allan, revised by Bob Bullock. *H.C.S. Bullock, His Life and Locomotives*. A to B Books, 2017.

Clayton, Howard. *The Duffield Bank & Eaton Railways*. Oakwood Press, 1968.

Croft, D.J. *A Survey of Seaside Miniature Railways*. Oakwood Press, 1992.

Heywood, Sir Arthur. *Heywood's Minimum Gauge Railways*. First printed in the 1890s, reprint by Scolar Press, 1974.

Holroyd, Dave, and Lawson Little. *The Locomotives of Severn-Lamb Ltd*. Narrow Gauge Railway Society, 2010.

Little, Lawson, and Dave Holroyd. *The Miniature Locomotives of David Curwen*. Narrow Gauge Railway Society, 2008.

Miniature Railway Magazine. (editor David Henshaw)

Steel, Ernest and Elenora Steel. *The Miniature World of Henry Greenly*. Model & Allied Publications, 1973.

Tebb, Dr Bob. *The Blakesley Miniature Railway and the Bartholomew Family*. Silver Link Publishing, 2009.

PLACES TO VISIT

Barnards Miniature Railway, Barnards Farm, Brentwood
Road, West Horndon, Essex CM13 3LX.
Website: www.barnardsminiaturerailway.eu.

Barton House Railway, Hartwell Road, The Avenue,
Wroxham, Norfolk NR12 8TL. Telephone 01603
782008. Website: www.bartonhouserailway.org.uk.

Beamish Cog Railway, Beamish Museum, Beamish, County
Durham DH9 0RG. Telephone: 0191 370 4000.
Website: www.beamish.org.uk.

Beer Heights Light Railway, Pecorama, Underleys, Beer,
Devon EX12 3NA.Telephone: 01297 21542.
Website: www.pecorama.co.uk.

Bickington Steam Railway, Trago Mills,
Newton Abbot, Devon TQ12 6JD.
Website: www.bickingtonrailway.wixsite.com.

Eastleigh Lakeside Railway, Lakeside Country Park, Wide
Lane, Eastleigh SO50 5PE. Telephone: 023 8061 2020.
Website: www.steamtrain.co.uk.

Great Cockcrow Railway, 4 Hardwick Lane, Chertsey
KT16 0AD. Telephone: 01932 565474.
Website: www.cockcrow.co.uk.

Hastings Miniature Railway, Rock-a-Nore Road,
Old Town, Hastings, East Sussex TN34 3DW.
Telephone: 07773 645228.

Lakeshore Railroad, South Marine Park, South Shields,
Tyne and Wear NE33 2NN. Telephone: 07745 350983.
Website: www.lakeshorerailroad.co.uk.

Moors Valley Country Park, Horton Road, Ashley Heath,
Dorset BH24 2ET. Telephone: 01425 470721.
Website: www.moors-valley.co.uk.

North Bay Railway, Northstead Manor Gardens,
Scarborough, North Yorkshire, YO12 6PF. Telephone:
01723 368791. Website: www.nbr.org.uk.

Ravenglass & Eskdale Railway, Ravenglass, Cumbria
  CA18 1SW. Telephone: 01229 717171.
  Website: www.ravenglass-railway.co.uk.

Romney, Hythe & Dymchurch Railway, New Romney
  Station, New Romney, Kent TN28 8PL. Telephone:
  01797 362353. Website: www.rhdr.org.uk.

South Downs Light Railway, Stopham Road Station,
  Pulborough Garden Centre, Pulborough, West Sussex
  RH20 1DS. Telephone: 07518 753784.
  Website: www.south-downs-railway.com.

Wells & Walsingham Light Railway, Wells-next-the-Sea,
  Norfolk NR23 1QB. Telephone: 01328 711630.
  Website: www.wwlr.co.uk.

Weston Park Miniature Railway, Weston-under-Lizard,
  Shifnal TF11 8LE. Telephone: 01952 852100.
  Website: www.weston-park.com.

Grandest of the new breed of 7¼-inch miniature railways is the line at Weston Park near Telford, which winds for 1¼ miles through a fine garden landscaped by Capability Brown.

INDEX

MINIATURE RAILWAYS

There are more than 400 miniature railways in Britain. Some are hidden away and privately owned, others are parkland attractions, and some – such as the Romney, Hythe and Dymchurch – comprise significant operations. They come in an array of gauges (from 5 inches up to 15 inches and sometimes greater), but their most definitive characteristic is that they can carry passengers, whether sitting astride the rolling stock or inside enclosed carriages. In this colourfully illustrated guide, David Henshaw offers a concise history of miniature railways from the nineteenth century to the modern day, including a whistle-stop tour of some of the most notable examples open to the public – such as the Ravenglass and Eskdale, Bure Valley and Eastleigh Lakeside railways – exploring their layouts, engineering and rolling stock.

David Henshaw has published several books on railways, bicycle technology and motoring, including *Apex: The Inside Story of the Hillman Imp*. He writes, edits, illustrates and distributes two specialist magazines: *A to B* and *Miniature Railway*.

www.shirebooks.co.uk

SHIRE PUBLICATIONS

ISBN 978-1-78442-440-4

5 1 4 0 0

9 781784 424404

www.shirebooks.co.uk

UK £8.99 | US $14.00 | CAN $19.00

WOMEN IN AVIATION

Julian Hale